Tilling the Soul

Isa N. Motley

PublishAmerica
Baltimore

© 2008 by Isa N. Motley.
All rights reserved. No part of this book may be reproduced, stored in a retrieval system or transmitted in any form or by any means without the prior written permission of the publishers, except by a reviewer who may quote brief passages in a review to be printed in a newspaper, magazine or journal.

First printing

ISBN: 1-60474-867-2
PUBLISHED BY PUBLISHAMERICA, LLLP
www.publishamerica.com
Baltimore

Printed in the United States of America

This book is dedicated to the memory of my dad
Mr. John Henry Motley, Jr.
09-27-1940 to 01-08-2005

Preface

In life we will all have different experiences with Love. We come from Love. We are Love. Our every existence evolves from Love. *Tilling the Soul* is a book about Love, while at the same time, it's a healing experience. My own experiences and thoughts about Love are reflected upon up to a certain point in my life within this collection. Love abounds greatly all around us. Being able to see that Love, witness that Love and appreciate that Love is a beautiful thing. I've found that not everyone feels Love. Not everyone has had the opportunity to know Love, as beautiful as it is. Love Lessons Won, Love Lessons Lost was almost the title of this piece. But then I had to think; there is no win or lose in Love. Understanding that there is no right or wrong when we engage in this thing called Love, we have many lessons. As long as we are learning from our lessons, we are always winning. Love is so many things. It bears no title. Love simply is. Often times we try to place boundaries on Love, boundaries that aren't relevant because Love does not fit under "subtitles". It does not live within boundaries. You can't place Love under limits. You can't be descriptive with Love and attempt to define it. Love simply is. Love is grander than you and me. Love is grander than an emotion, any that we may feel. We may be moved to many emotions while experiencing Love. We may feel like we're passing or we're failing while we feel as though we're being tested, when simply we should be learning and appreciating the opportunity to experience Love, again, having no right or wrong, but realizing, there is a lesson that we each must learn. Life is a series of lessons. Love is many engagements with lessons attached. Love is so many things we should never dare try to give it a title. Love just is.

Inspired greatly by four individuals, many of these pieces have helped mature me as an individual in understanding that Love simply is. You should never be upset if someone does not Love you the way you feel as though you should be Loved. Your journey with that individual may be over, true enough, be it good or bad. But remember, no two people will ever Love the same. No two people will ever experience Love the same. We should never "expect" another to Love us as we Love. Expecting to be Loved and feel Loved as we feel we give Love is when we set ourselves up to feel as though we are "winning" or "losing" at Love, when Love simply is. As we learn to simply enjoy the beauty in everything and everyone, we will learn to respect and appreciate the Love that is in everything and everyone. Love abounds in all things. The more we concentrate and focus on exuding Love, the more Love will come our way. The more we till our souls, the more we allow good seeds to be planted, and we can reap the abundant harvest of Love. *Tilling the Soul* will take you on a journey of emotional healing and spiritual growth. It has allowed me and it will allow you the opportunity to appreciate Love in its every form. I hope that you will be inspired to allow yourselves to be completely healed from any old wounds that you've allowed to fester and manifest within and begin to turn over all of the negative energies that will and can prevent you from growing, all of the negative energies that prevent us from enjoying the experiences of Love.

Be Blessed and Be Love.

—Isa N. Motley

If Tomorrow Never Comes

If tomorrow never comes
I'm happy for today
And I'll do my best to make the most of it
If tomorrow never comes
I'm not mad at all about yesterday
Because I'm still looking forward to tomorrow
If this should be my last chance to see the sun shine
I want the best view
So it can shine as bright as it can on me
As the moon descends to rest
And I'm waiting for my morning kiss by the brightest star in the sky
I'll listen as the birds sing a song for me
If tomorrow never comes
I want to see each hue in nature
Just a tad bit different than I did the day before
Appreciate how the blue in the sky
Complements the green leaves on the trees
Which is all beautifully reflected by my sun
If tomorrow never comes
I'm happy for today
Because I still have a chance to see the differences
In all of mankind
I still have a chance to truly appreciate the struggles we all fight to overcome
I still have a chance to learn
Smiling more today than yesterday
I'll be more sincere in all I do and say

Appreciating beauty all around me in every form
If tomorrow never comes
I'm happy for today
And I'll do my best to make the most of it
If tomorrow never comes
I'm not mad at all about yesterday
Because I'm still looking forward to tomorrow
But tonight
Should tomorrow choose not to come
I want my love to be felt
Just one more time
I want to feel love
Just one more time
I want to make love
Just one more time
I want my baby
To be my friend
To be my lover
Just one more time
Tonight
I want us to talk like we've never talked before
I want us to touch like we've never touched before
I want us to taste like we've never tasted before
I want us to love like we've never loved before
I want to be held like tomorrow might not come
I want to kiss taking advantage of each second we have
Now
And if tomorrow should choose not to come
I won't be mad about today
Because I've made the most of it
But
If I close my eyes to sleep
Thankful for all that I was blessed with today

And wake to another morning kiss
By the brightest star in the sky
Today will begin tomorrow
And I'll do my best to make the most of it
I still won't be mad about yesterday
Because I'll still be looking forward to tomorrow
But I know for some
Tomorrow never came today
For some
Tomorrow won't come tomorrow
So for me today
I'm going to live like tomorrow may not come
I won't procrastinate today
Because
Today is my tomorrow which was my yesterday
Today

Never Give Up

Each day I rise I have to thank you
Opportunity awaiting
Each day I rise I have to thank you
I'm never giving up
I'm never giving in
The same tune same song some may see
Not when the birds sing a little differently
Not when my focus is becoming a little clearer
I'm never giving up
I'm never giving in
We have 365 days to start over in one year
365 chances to get "it" right
Boundless opportunities for one's destiny to surface
To material existence
If you press for the mark
How could I give up?
How could I give in?
The sky seems a touch bluer today
Or is just my determination a degree keener?
Everyone's hello a taste politer
My intensity marked on a Richter Scale
Reaching near the highest level possible
Tenacious velocity to excel
Persevering always
Because
I'm never giving up
I'm never giving in
How could I when it's been embedded in me since I was a child

By the one who masterfully created us all?
The world is yours
The amount of opportunity awaiting you is unlimited
You can create
Whatever you can envision
All I had to do is dream
All you have to do is dream
Forget who you are today
Remember who you were
Forget where you are
Remember where you came from
Don't go to sleep
DREAM
We're all Destined for Riches
We've always been destined
Create your destiny
Is what I remembered
I didn't give up!
I didn't give in!
I'm living my DREAM.

Today

I can't take back yesterday
Like the dust in the wind after a Monsoon
My mind is spinning
Confused
Trying to figure out how we went from
Happy to sad
I need a psychotherapist to analyze this relation
Ships come and go like the seconds in a day
Hourglasses tilt
The second hand
Tick
Tocks
My relationships play a mind game
But I still can't take back yesterday
Now, racing
I'm beginning to feel like Jeff Gordon
Trying to figure out what I did wrong
Never
The mind comes up with its own perception of right and wrong
And still trying to take back yesterday
I realize
I'm slowly drifting into tomorrow in yesterday mode
Grasping reality for what it is
I've come to realize
I need to change
Today

To Be Continued

To be where you are
She wished she could be
Peaceful
Tranquil
Tearless
Free of all her pain
Sadness made life so hard
Her days long
Nights endless
Morning came bringing with it new hope
She had so many questions the night before
Questions that I had no answers to
Why did she have me if she hated me so
I'm sure then abortions were legal
To doom a child should constitute a felony
Life behind bars without parole
That's what she tries to do to my soul
Is what she told me
Fighting to get out behind each teardrop that falls
My soul now feels captured
Just as hers had last night
Why was she left here to feel such pain
Fighting
To be set free
Free from the bondage of those that slighted her
"I just want it all to end," were the last words she spoke
Before I woke up from my dream.

Through My Pen

I speak truth to you through my pen
My soul opens up
While I converse with myself through my brain
I allow the world to experience a taste of Isa
So many thoughts
No one to tell
So many feelings
No one to share
So much love
No one to hold
Alone
But so full
Like each great body of water that runs deep
Strategically placed
I am in many lives
So many have taken from me what they needed
Never questioning if what I needed was received in return
Such is life
Again, I speak truth to you through my pen
As my soul continues to open up
Lonely
Never
For I share my world with many
Fulfilled
Not
For I am lonely
You might ask
Does that make sense?

Much

A lack of companionship can bring about many lonely feelings
While talking to countless
Meaningful and meaningless conversations in a day
Am I sharing with someone who wants to willingly share back?
Am I loving someone who wants to love back?
Am I opening up and exploring another's mind
While I allow myself to be open and explored?
I still speak truth to you through my pen
As my soul continues to open up
Watching the sunset over still waters
Such a beautiful sight
Peaceful and relaxed
I reminisce on beautiful times I've had
Times I've felt absolutely loved
And times I let slip away
That bitter pill called regret is a hard one to swallow
When you wake up each day to someone who truly does not deserve
Someone who truly does not care
Someone you've let your beautiful times
Slip away for
And they haven't a clue about enjoying your sunset
As golden as it is
As I continue to speak truth to you through my pen
And my soul continues to open up
I feel helpless to my desires
Yearning for one touch
One touch is the only touch
That will ease me
His touch
Is the one touch
That pleases me

I close my eyes and it's his face I see
Brown skin
Chocolate so deep
Chestnut eyes that scream
I Love You
Each time they see me
Lips that say
I want to taste you
While my body experiences pleasures only he can bring me
Truth to you I speak
Through my pen
Open is my soul

Faultless She'll Be When She's Gone

She can't believe she left home for this
She can't believe she gave it all up for this
She can't believe she believed what he spoke was truth
She can't believe she believed
When she already knows that real is hard to find
To encounter a being that's empty inside is a sad encounter
She had never seen in all of her life someone so selfish
Someone so cold and empty
Looking deep into their eyes takes you into darkness
Never
In all of her days
Would she have imagined…
Could she have imagined…
She'd spend a part of her life in such existence
How does one grow so cold
So heartless
So empty?
Demons trying to suck life out of her core being
A failed attempt
Wishing she'd never had to be witness to such a life
A testament she now has for many
A testament of sadness
A testament of loneliness
A testament of pain
A testament of sorrow
A testament of tried faith
A testament of prevailing
She's overcome demon forces

She will overcome any demonic spirit that's been cast into others
Others that lack the faith
Others that lack the power
Others that lack the Holy Spirit that's greater than any spirit
Others that have failed to realize that they too
Can be free
Consumed with darkness left by many generations before
She can't fight demonic spirits in others and risk her own soul
She can't fight his demons
She wouldn't
Especially when she can't see he's fighting
Especially when all she could witness is comfort with his being
Comfort with the coldness
Comfort with the solitude and sadness
The pain evident
When you're allowed to look into his eyes
Especially when all she can witness is contentment
Contentment with the sword that had been wedged between them
Is it easier secluding yourself when you know
Deep inside
Your fight with your inner demons is not turning into a triumphant
battle
A victory for the enemy because you're scared to fight
Scared of what lies ahead
Scared to face your demons
Scared to come face to face with your past
Overcome with fear you succumb to loneliness
Is it easier to just be empty
Emotionless
Heartless
Cold?
She can't believe she left home for this
She can't believe she gave it all up for this

Everything she had
She can't believe she believed what he spoke was truth
She can't believe she believed
When she already knows that real is hard to find
Masking behind coldness
Fronting behind a heart made of stone
Empty completely inside
This is not what she's made of
This is not what she came from
Not even her worst of times
Faultless she'll be when she's gone

Clueless

You can never do enough for someone
Not when they think the world owes them everything
Why I insist on trying to make those happy
Who are so undeserving of my love
I don't know
I used to think as long as I'm giving my all
It will eventually be reciprocated
However
I'm much wiser in my beliefs now
Still I insist on attracting an area within myself
That is so far from being complete and whole
An area within myself
That obviously feels indebted to trials and tribulations
Because that is all I manage to receive from these worthless acquaintances
Why I subject myself to unprecedented attractions
When I know so much is to be desired
There's so much more that can be offered
I haven't a clue...

Katrina

Built by man
Engineered by a strong mind
It's in my blood
Instinctively I've got to survive
The best way I know how suits me
To you I might be prissy
Even a little naïve to myself and to others
But at the core of this frame
Is a heart built for hustlin'
And a soul ready to flow
Give me the situation
And automatically like Simon Says
I'm adding and subtracting
Multiplying and dividing
After figuring out what $X \times Y$ will equal
I'll tell you my next move
Who cares if it's not your cup of tea?
Who cares if Adam bit the apple because Eve was on the top of her game?
It's my world and it's my nut
If you don't want to be like Adam, it's okay
But like Eve
I plan to be on top
Ridin' until this race is over
Given up ain't in my blood
To settle for less than I know this world has to offer is for the meek and passive
Less aggressive individual

Like Queen Nefertiti
I must reign
Mistakes; I've made many which helped me to
Re-Member's only
Is the name of my club
Who I was is who I be
A queen, ready to rule if her king steps down
Ready to have his back if he exists
Ready to ride-or-die if he so orders
Hustlin' and Flowin'
It's in my blood
Built for battle
Ready for war

Because of You

Because of you
Never again will I settle
The world can call me what they want
But I know I can do better
Because of you
I am able to see clearly now
Superficial qualities that are truly non-existent
Because of you
I no longer lack the self-esteem that's been deep within me all along
The drive and determination
That's backing my profound motivation
Because of you
I know I am going to make it to the top
I am able to see the stars that shine brightly
A reflection of the fire that's burning in me
Because of you
My desires have changed
What drives me to meet each challenge with raw determination
Raw perseverance…
Raw ambition…
Is knowing…
Knowing life is all about choices
Decisions we make
Because of you I am able to see clearly now
Blinded by all of the molecules and neurons
The epidermis and chromosomes
That surround us every day

I am able to see past the physical and connect with the spiritual
Because of you
I know there are "No Substitutions"
Never again will I settle...
Happiness is a gift we can each decide to open or keep wrapped
Exuding from each pore on my body I want the entire world to see
What Happiness and Joy lives inside of me
Because of you
My outlook on life has changed
Perceiving it to have some correlation with another's
I now know it is what you make it
Our chapters are written by us
We set the stage, write the script and live the scenes...
Changing characters if they don't fit
Because of you some chapters are done...
Because of you
Never again will I settle
The world can call me what they want...
I know I can do better

Everlasting Love

Beginning each day with thoughts of you
And ending each with the same
It's called Everlasting Love
You gave me so much
And you had so much more to give
I suppose this lifetime could not encompass
All that you had within
Missing you each day is the hardest thing in the world for me
I feel like my soul has been lifted out of my body
Leaving just a hollow shell
Walls closing in on me
I just want to hold your hand
To kiss your forehead just one more time
Is one of many thoughts
Constantly running through my mind
I think of the day you left me
Replaying each second
All 2,937,600 of them
Those last 34 days
Up to that very one…
The one that left me fatherless…
The one that took my daddy away…
The one that reminds me with each tear that falls…
I don't know how I'm going to go on without you
It's called Everlasting Love
That's what you gave me…
That's why this emptiness feels like a paperweight on my heart
No one has ever loved me like you

And never can your love be replaced
Yes I've been loved before
It's true...
This I can say with much confidence
I was "Daddy's Little Girl" for 33 years
Then someone needed you more than me
Your comforting spirit that eased all worries and pain
Your smile that warmed my heart
Your laugh was infectious
Like honey to a bee
I hear it in my mind and keep it on auto-replay always
All of the good times along with the bad
I want them back
If only for an hour
I want to turn back the hands of time
If only for a minute
I'd like to hit rewind
If only for a second I could see your face
I'd whisper in your ear, "Daddy,
I'll never forget."
You gave me Everlasting Love.

Nothing but Love

To know I've hurt you makes me sad
You fill my heart with such joy
You are the reason for the sparkle in my eyes
The smile that graces my face daily
Is in part because of the thoughts you've implanted deep inside me…
What we began so long ago
Has never left my heart
Your eyes speak so many languages to me
Many not understood
Yet, when I look deep
The passion that fills them is so familiar
We started something that is rare
Precious like the jewels found at the very bottom of the deepest ocean
How I could have ever doubted your love
Only confirms what I've come to realize to be truth
I was scared…
To find someone who's willing to be as real as you
Willing to express the love they have for you exposing the real them
Willing to feel your pain with you because they love you just that much
Willing to risk it all to be by your side
To find someone who knows who they are and what they want
Is rare…
As rare as the love we found so long ago that never went away
To find someone who's willing to let you do you

Until he asks
Will you marry me?
And you say, "Se"
'Cause for real, he don't want to be he
Not without his ye yi
To find someone who is willing to make
You + Me = We
Only equates to one thing…
Destiny
This leads to my known truth;
I was scared
We became us so long ago
But then you went away
When love said hello to me again
I said, "Hi,"
But I was shy
I embraced you with half a heart
Playing Russian roulette with my poker face on
Taking chances with what I knew was destiny
Taking chances when I knew what I felt was real
Taking chances when I could see clearly
Each time I looked deep into your eyes…
That what you felt for me was Nothing but Love…

Things Just Aren't the Same…

Things just aren't the same
Since you went away
Yeah the sun still comes out
After the night fades to day
My eyes tear with the thought though
That the rays just don't feel the same
Since you left nothing seems to ease our pain
Nothing warms my heart the way your smile did
How I'd give anything just to be able to hear you say
Just one more time,
"Hey, kid,"
But now you're gone
And that just won't happen anymore
And no one seems to understand why…
I cry endlessly behind closed doors
Things just aren't the same
Since you went away
Except for one fact that will always remain…
We Love You Dad…

Electric

It's been electric since day one
I fight hard to control the way my body yearns for him when he's not near
Urges to touch myself consume me
He touches my body the way it's never been touched
Overwhelmed by this constant smog-like desire I have for him
How will I ever be able to let him go?
I court the fact that he sets me on fire inside
Mind, Body & Soul…
I'm as free as a bird in the wind when I'm with him
It's absurd…the very thought of losing him…
Not my lover…
Not my friend…
It's absurd that…what we just began has to end
But it's still so electric
The passion we have for one another
The longing that's secreted from our pores
Mine smells like him…
His smell like me…
Intense Eroticism is what I'd call it if I could bottle it and sell it in a store
But I can't…
It's something that is shared between the two of us
I feel like a dope fiend
And *only* he is my fix
But I'm constantly reminded that…
I gotta let him go
Regardless to how bad the shit hurts…

Even if it is still electric
I'm constantly reminded that…
He's somebody else's man and…
What we tried to begin definitely has to end and…
Ain't nothing goin' on between us for real but sin and
I can't win in sin…
Even if he is my friend
Constant smog-like desire or not till the end…
Even if it is still electric
I'm constantly reminded that…
I gotta let him go…

Does It Mean Anything?

Does it mean anything?
The way you hold me when you love me
The way you pull away when you want to be near
Does any of it mean anything
When you want to be somewhere else
Anywhere
But here?...
How can I love someone who wants to be with someone else?
It's killing me trying to search my soul for the answer
Nowhere inside of me it seems
Am I able to justify what is transpiring between us
My mind is perplexed
How could I sacrifice everything?
How could you allow me to give you my all
My every being...everything I am...
Only to meet doubt and regret not two months later?
You see just a short while ago
I was your sun by day...
Your stars by night...
I was the air you longed to breathe...
The food you desired to taste...
Now today I'm nothing
So easily you can toss me to the side
As if none of this existed
Was any of it ever real? is my question
Did any of it ever mean anything to you?
Because right now if you were to answer me,
"Yes,"

I would reply,
"Bullshit."
I feel like what we had was a 180-night stand
Which lead to you doing a complete 360° on me
And when you break the shit all the way down
It amounts to nothing
How can nothing mean something if nothing does not even exist?
It can't...
So you see...I'm sorry if you find that
Love doesn't live here anymore...
How can I love someone who wants to be with someone else?
None of it was ever real...
None of it meant anything...apparently
To you...

Mistakes

What do you do when you know you've made a mistake?
Twice so far in life I've had it all
And thrown it away
Will the Lord forgive me for being so blind?
I pray…
For once…
My eyes are open
I cry endlessly for my life back
But…
Never again will it be the same
Reality hitting home I've realized that
I once was loved
What I thought was not right
What I once prayed for to end
Is…
What I now pray for
What I couldn't wait to get out of…
Is what I want back
If only I could turn back the hands of time
Happiness would find shelter
Inside this shell of a heart I behold
Loneliness creeping in
I just want to hear the words
"I Love You"
Even if I do think they're without validation
How could I have been so blind
Tormented by visions of what used to be?
I can't believe today

My life has no meaning
What do you do when you know you've made a mistake?
Dear Lord, I just want my life back…

What Kind of Fool Am I

How can I still want him
When I know he's chosen another
Craving for his touch
His lips desire to be on hers
My heart is in agony because
I Love him...
My eyes are full of tears
Simply because I Love him...
Torn between two women
I still allow him to feel my warmth
Riding him...and loving every bit
Does he fantasize of her? I wonder
Maybe for a split second even see her...
Why has my love ended so suddenly?
How could I not see it coming?
Blinded and completely caught off guard
I let down my defenses
Now I try to disguise all this pain
Playing a game of charades with no one but myself
I'm not even deluded
It's funny...
I know what time it is and...
I can't even be mad long enough for crying and...
I can't stop crying because I'm mad
And sad...
And crying...
And slowly dying it seems
It's crazy because I never would have thought we would be ending

like this
Call me delusional
But somehow I thought this was going to last
Maybe it was the way he held me and kissed me
The first time
Maybe it was when he told me he loved me
Or when he said he wanted to be mine…
Perhaps it was simply the way he looked deep into my eyes
As he held me close
I don't know because everything happened so fast
And now it's all a big blur
All that's left behind
All that I have left to hold on to
Is this empty feeling that I carry with me every day
In spite of it all
I still want this man…
I still love this man…
What kind of fool am I?

This poem is dedicated to the memory of my dad John Henry Motley, Jr. (a.k.a. "Thunder")

Never Say Goodbye

Never say, "Goodbye,"
It will always be, "See you later."
I'll catch up with you in a better place
Beyond the stars you went to be
Pathing the way for those you left behind
We'll keep it tight
Holding things down just as you taught us
Forever carrying you in our hearts
You've taught so many so much
Making lasting impressions
Impressions that will never go away
100% you were
No matter what the role was you had to lead
No validation is needed…
You were all man
An excellent husband…
An excellent dad…
An excellent example…
Of the type of man to be
An excellent example
Of the type of person to be
One with a pure heart
You were genuine
Towards all you came in contact with
Never putting on any false visages

You were always real
Instilling values and morals in us
That a blind man could see
To find another whose love was sincere always
Whose caring took precedence
Over whether we were right or wrong
Whose encouragement was never with limitations
To find another would take a lifetime
But no other could ever take your place
You had true Agape love
Love unconditional with no constraints
You knew the real meaning
And hopefully you were able to teach those
Who claim to know
What love is all about
You never simply said, "I Love You"
You showed it in all you did and said
Your actions always spoke louder than your words
You never said, "Goodbye,"
Knowing we would always be together
In spirit you are and forever will be with me
With us…
It will never ever be, "Goodbye"
One day we will see you later…
I Love You…

The Good Times

When, Where, and Why
When will they return?
Where did they go?
Why?
The Good Times...
When everyone had smiles on their faces
You could feel the love in the room
Smell it in the air
The Good Times...
When all the family was there
Plenty of food
And laughter to take care of the worst ailment
The times you never got enough of
Days that turned into nights then greeted us with daylight again
Cards slappin' on tables
Dominoes breakin'
Kids running playing hide-and-go-seek
The Good Times...
When you cried and laughed
Laughed and cried
The times when no one ever wanted to say goodbye
The Good Times...

It's More Than Simply Love

I don't know why lately you've been on my mind
I've given my heart to another and what we had is over
Yet
When I close my eyes it's your face I see
Your face…
Your smile…
Your walk…
I hear your laugh
I can still smell your scent
It's disturbing me because I know it's him I desire
Yet you're constantly creeping into my thoughts
Just like the thief that stole my heart and soul before
I can't imagine what part of me is still stuck on what was so long ago
When I have such happiness before me now
Today I have a man who loves me…
I stare out into nowhere and I have so many vivid pictures
Flooding my brain
Memories that seem like they won't disappear
Yet today I have a man who loves me…
I have a man who loves me…
I had a man who loved me…
I am a woman and I love me…
I love me and today I no longer want a man to love me…
Not just to simply love me…
I want to be loved…
I want to feel love…
I want to create—define—a new love…
The type of love that will carry me across miles that seem endless

Yet
I don't care about the journey
The type of love where all I can seem to do is wish he was here
Or I was there
Because the distance—any amount—is driving me crazy
The type where I can feel his breath on my skin through the phone lines
Smell his scent
As if electricity is carrying it across the miles just for my nose
The type of love that has chills running through my body as I taste his lips
The type that makes me wish I were magic
So that I could become transparent and ease through the phone lines
And into his arms
With miles on miles between us
And as my mind carries me across each one
All I can think about is the type of love we're going to make
Once the miles disappear
Today…I have a man who loves me
Now when I close my eyes and see your face
I still see your smile…
I see your walk…
I hear your laugh…
I can still smell your scent even…
And it's no longer disturbing because
I'm reminded of
The love that I knew I deserved
The type of love I knew I desired
The love that I've found today…
Today I have a man who loves me
I have a man whose smile warms me up
Like a cup of cocoa on a cold winter's day

Whose touch can ease all my pains away
Today I have a man whose kiss lifts me past cloud #9
A man who is willing to make his heart, his love and his name, be all mine
Today I have more than a man who simply loves me
Today, tomorrow and for the rest of our days
We will be in love…

Untitled

I don't know what it is...
Maybe it's the way his smile slowly appears across his face...
Lips moist like the inside of my thighs
With each thought of him now
Where did these feelings come from?
I don't know what it is
Perhaps it's the way he looks at me
Knowing I've been looking at him
Eyes fixed in amazement at what appears to be the beginning of forever
Forever and the beginning of beautiful days and nights we have to spend together
Silently
Learning each other it feels like he's been around me already, but I know we just met
I know he does not know for sure yet that
I'm dying to taste him all over
Starting with his lips that hypnotize me each time he speaks
He does not know for sure yet that
I know he's dying to taste me all over
Starting with whatever sweet spot he can get to first
How can it be I long for this man so and our forever just began yesterday?
It feels like magnets were secretly placed within our bodies
And we were drawn to one another
Secretly we were set up for what destiny already knew existed
I feel my energy in him each time he's near
And when he's gone I know something's missing

He is
My other half
You see I am he and he is I and together we create we which equals our destiny
A destiny that had a beautiful beginning
One which has nothing short of incredible for the ending
You see this is what he does to me
This man that appeared and I don't know what it is
Maybe it was the way his smile slowly appeared across his face
That resulted in no one else being able to take his place…

Love Junkie

Maybe it's because he's who he is
Maybe it's because I can't stop thinking about him
Maybe it's because I keep having this thought that he and I were meant to be
I'm really not sure if it's love or if it's a strong case of like
All I know is
I want him bad
It's almost like being hungry and you can smell the food
Taste it even
Yet there's no food around
He's in my spirit and my soul
His face painted in my left cranium
His smell…touch…taste in my right
I'm crazy about this man and there's nothing anyone can do about it
Good or bad
Right or wrong
I've got to have him near me
I've got to feel his touch
At least once more
Perhaps for life—no one knows
Right now I know I need a fix and he's my dope
A junkie for him
His love…
His smile…
The things he does…
I am…
A love junkie

Goodbye…

You said she was the one
Well excuse me but I didn't know chivalry was dead
Had I known I doubt I would have let you in my bed
You see I'm a lady and right now I want to be the first to say, "Goodbye."
I'm sure I'll be the only one who might cry
I want to reminisce on how
So you said
I was the only one who didn't forget your birthday
But evidently the only one who forgot to ask you out on a date
Huh, maybe I'm a little slow here but it's just not adding up in my book
You didn't look like a player but somehow I feel like I got took
You played a shrewd game and I can't even be mad at you
It's just that I don't like how now I question if anything you said was true
You seemed like a gentleman
The perfect man for a lady
Or perhaps a chameleon on the down-low
With his hands in a lil' bit of this and a lil' bit of that
Maybe?
Sometimes I ponder had my dreams come true where I would now be?
If my past life as I saw it would currently be my present
What would be different?
Who would still be around?
And how different would my relations be
Had I foreseen the reality of my world through a dream?

Would you simply have been a mirage?
Is it that while I'm trying to get next to you and feel you a lil' bit
You really aren't there to get next to or be felt?
Or could it be that the gentleman is there
He's just not in you?
You had me faked out…
Now this is truth!
I wanted to be the first to say, "Goodbye,"
But right now Goodbye doesn't even matter
We both know it's over, and there's really no sense in wishing on a four-leaf clover
What we had was good while it lasted
But right now our love affair is simply a thing of the past
Chivalry is not dead it's just a quality you don't possess
I'm starting to wonder if you really are cold and heartless
I know you've been hurt before
At least that's what you told me
But so have I you see
And hurt gives you no reason to lie
I believe in karma
I know it to be a true thing
And what you put out into the universe comes back to you a full 180°
As I stare into your eyes I see such depth
Eyes that once gave passageway to a soul that's since left
Eyes that had me caught up in believing a mirage
Believing what was fake was real when really what I thought was real was fake
Eyes that had been captured by a chameleon that had been playing with my heart
Eyes that I'm saying goodbye to now and should have from the start…
Goodbye…

Ready or Not

She kept telling herself
He is not the one for you
You don't have to be second choice for anyone
But somehow this situation manifested itself that
Truly did not reflect who she was
Knowing she should be number one
How could she continue to go on acknowledging that
Truly she was not the one he wished to spend his time with
Publicly
Yeah, an hour or two behind closed doors where…
No one that exists even matters
To get just a feel of the warmth—that's like sunny skies on a cloudy day
And the sweetness—that's like caramel or hot fudge being poured on top of a sundae
That's in between her thighs
Yeah that's okay…
And it will continue to be as long as she says it is
But for real…naw she's not the one
How she allowed herself to get involved in this love triangle…
This love octagon…
This dreaded illusion of love…
She doesn't know
Situations like this should make you question yourself as a person
What's incomplete about me?
Analyzing the situation and viewing it for what it was allowed her to determine that
What she had was a love affair

With someone who was truly incomplete in many areas of his life
That's why he needed so many **flavors,** I'll say, of women
To make him feel complete
That's why he played so many different roles
Truly he was not ready for her or anything she stood for when it came to male/female relations
Yeah he could sex her down good
But was he ready to go deep; deep into her soul?
Could his soul meet mine and spark a blue flame
The kind that's way hot
Or must we keep this superficial to keep him comfortable?
Is what she questioned
Maybe she should pose these questions to him
Or maybe she should just keep things the way they are; knowing who she is
He's the only one who might get caught up trying to cum up in her when for real, he's not even ready
Not like she's ready
Ready to explore his mind
Ready to go deep into his body and soul
Places he may not be ready for another to explore
Places he keeps hidden behind many faces
Faces that may or may not be
Ready…

Insanity

My perception of what was real was clouded by tender kisses
Reality seeping through
While I was drowning in fantasy of having something
Something not belonging to me in the first place
Denying to myself he loved others the same way he loved me
Denying to myself he had left others feeling the same way he left me
Denying to myself he was the man my mama warned me about all along
I continued to indulge in what was not the best decision making on my part
I continued to see a man that I knew was toxic to my mental state-of-mind
Insanity is when you continue to do something over and over
Achieving the same result
Yet I continued on my roller coaster ride with this man
Straddling sanity and insanity
Because each time I went up, I came back down…
With the same feeling
That I had to be insane…

In a Zone

I wonder if ever my skies will be blue
Will darkness fade into light?
My smile is resting
Not completely turned upside down
But all the color is gone from my picture
I see hills with grass
Not green
Not brown
I see trees with leaves
I don't know if they're alive or dead
My vision is focused
It's just neutral
How does one come to such a place?
Traumatic to have life come to this
No feeling
Numb
I want to feel
I can't allow myself
No black or white
Just grey
I want to see life
It's just not a safe place for me now
Too many games
Too much pain
Afraid of what's on the next level
It's safer for me this way
I often wonder what sent OJ over the edge
Relating is worse than wonderment
Knowing you're not ready
It's safer to stay in a zone…

Where Do We Go from Here?

Where do we go from here?
How long must we say, "Goodbye"?
If I had to look into an hourglass
Would I see your face in the sands of time?
In my mirror your reflection is stained
Looking back at me
Gazing with eyes that are as deep as the River Nile
I'm lost in imagination
While envisioning the last time we made love
Transcending in time
I'm taken back and close to ecstasy with the very thought of your body and mine touching
Where do we go from here?
When we've gone so many places
I've played many parts and I've been many things
But never before have I fallen so soon so fast for anyone
Scared to loose you
I have no choice but to let go
And I just don't know
Where we go from here
With me you'll always be
In my dreams I can feel you kissing my lips softly
Sending me on a natural high with the slightest taste of your tongue
Mentally you're here with me
Taking me to new plateaus
Arousing my intellect with your signature choice of words
I don't know who can compare to you physically
Because even now with the very thought of you lovin' me I

practice my Kegels
Trying to tame the fire burning within while I feel myself moisten
Wishing you were here inside of me...
I don't know how I'm going to do it
And I keep asking myself the same questions over and over in my head...
Where do we go from here?
Where will you go?
Where will I go?
What will I do?
Who will you do?

The First Time

I never would have imagined that seeing him for the first time
My feelings would grow like they have
Knowing he belonged to another and knowing my heart was fragile
I always knew in my mind we could never be more than "friends"
How do two friends cross the line then easily or suddenly let go?
When does love hit you dead smack in the face and you see it coming
Or must it always take you by surprise?
These are questions I've been asking myself since meeting him
Pertinent questions to a situation I opened myself up to not knowing if I was ready
Questions that have no right or wrong answer
Questions that really require no answer because an answer won't change the fact…
I've met someone who has changed my life
Since I've allowed him into my life
No answer can change the fact that I've met a man…
Yearned for a man…
Had passion-filled eyes for a man…
Loved a man with my heart…body…and soul…
All within three months
Is there an answer for why it's come to this, us giving each other our last kiss?
Is there an answer for my knowing soon all I'll have left to do is reminisce?
About what feels so right
I never would have imagined seeing him for the first time
I would come to long for him so

Knowing soon he must go...
And it all happened within three short months
No one can convince me that what we started was not real...
That what I feel in my heart is not true...
That what I see in his eyes as he looks deep into mine
Is not a man longing for the love he feels from me...
A man wanting to feel something real...
Something right...
There's no answer for why I don't want to let go
Time has a way of bringing about change
Things and occurrences in life we often times don't understand
However for us all
The inevitable must and will happen
For none of us possess the power to stop such a process
Time has brought about many changes for me...
Most recently healing for my fragile heart
I've met a man who reminded me that love does feel good
Who reminded me why I've always believed in Romeo and Juliet...
The type of love Shakespeare wrote about so passionately
I've met a man that brought a sparkle back into my eyes...
And I never would have imagined seeing him for the first time
I would have developed all these different feelings and emotions so soon...
Now we must say goodbye...
Knowing all things happen for a reason...
There's a purpose for our whole situation
In knowing this with each thought of him I smile...
Memories we created will forever be with me...
Keeping a flame ignited deep within...
Goodbye for us won't be forever...
Simply until our First Time occurs again...

Crying

Crying, Crying, Crying
I'm crying inside
And no one even knows
I'm dying inside
Does anyone even care?
Can you see my unhappiness when you look at me?
It's evident and always there
Are you looking?
Can't you see?
The trails of tears that follow me…

Never Again

Sometimes sitting thinking
I can't help but to go there
A place only you and I shared
People don't understand what I see
They can't understand why
The very thought of you makes my heart tug
Tears form just thinking
You and I will never be again
How can I love you to the very core of my existence
And still want you with all of my being
Yet know you're so wrong for me?
No one will ever understand
What you do for me
Only God knows I breathe every day
Longing for you
Wanting the key to turn and see your face enter through my door
A dark place I've entered since you've been gone
Pain hidden behind a smile
Because my baby is gone
The only man I truly love
Is just a memory within
No one on this earth can know
That it is you that makes me complete
Only your touch can ease the pain
But I vowed never again…

Irregular Heart Rhythms

This feeling I get when I think of you excites me so
To the point where
Irregular Heart Rhythms I'd swear I was having
Never before have I felt so free
Free to be me
I have you to thank
You have truly come into my life
Once more
And changed my world completely
Each day I wake I smile just as the sun
After a long night's sleep
Anxious to show the world a jewel has awakened
A void you have filled in my life
In my heart
I must thank you because you've come and brought so much joy to my world
Just as a butterfly evolving from its cocoon
Captive once was my heart
You have taught me how to love again
Showing me the difference between true happiness and what's fake
My life has forever changed since the beginning of you and me
Clouds that once hovered over my spirit are gone
Angie Stone said it best
"My sunshine has come and I'm all cried out; there's no more rain in these clouds."
Precipitation expected is zero
It's a new day in my camp and I owe it all to you

Eternal gratitude is yours from me to you
I'll forever carry you in my heart
Feeling like I've been baptized in a sea of love
I've consumed so much that it's manifested itself for the world to see
A real and true kind of love
With feelings reciprocated
That's what we share
I often imagine how it would be if we were alone
Just you and I and the air we would breathe
You know sometimes the greatest celebrations are the quietest
Tonight let me hear your heartbeat
I often dream of times we'd spend alone
Imagining the flickering of flames from candles lit
Providing music for our ears
That night we would be celebrating us
Me and you
You and I
The air between our bodies will be played like a keyboard as we make love
Making sure to hit each note perfectly
We come together, like a jigsaw puzzle
As the wind blows
Silk curtains will flow
The breeze will feel heavenly as it gently caresses our nude bodies
I can hear the desire and longing we have for each other
The volume getting louder and louder
As I silently crave for you to play me like a guitar
The thumping of my heartbeat provides a solo for us
Our senses are aroused by the keenest of pleasures
Such as you blowing on my neck ever so lightly
I think to myself
What a beautiful melody we've created

Our notes cascading like a waterfall
The audience within both our minds screams for an encore
This feeling I get excites me so
Tonight I know
I'm having Irregular Heart Rhythms…

Killing Me Softly

Right now she's not really understanding her feelings
All she knows is
It pains her to see him with another
It pains her not to have him there with her
Although he wasn't there when they had a home
It pains her
Not to have him by her side while she tries to be strong
Strong for both herself and her family
If nothing else she now knows his strength was there
Even when he was not
She's missing him so much I think its killing her inside
Does she dare tell another
How the only man that she's ever allowed to completely know her
inside and out
The man that she longed to bear children with
Who claimed to love her
But not enough to give her the greatest gift God has ever given
mankind—birth—
Who abused her
But still got all her love
Does she dare tell another that he now sits with a woman with
eight children
But she could not get one?
Does she dare tell that she still loves him so
But not enough to go back?
Does she dare tell how she still cries because she's lonely
Experiencing a different type of loneliness?
Before she did still have someone to call her own

Although he shared himself with others
He came home to her
It's funny then that was not enough
Now she wonders…would it be if…
But she never completes the thought
She wants to cry each time she sees him
She finds herself daydreaming more than she has in years
Why was she not enough?
But he flaunts her around like he's won a prize
She laughs truly to keep from crying
As she sits waiting on the doctors to call her
They need to check for tumors that may be growing inside
She sits all alone
All she can think is would he care if he knew?
Would he be here with me if he knew?
How could this be after almost two decades?
How could she question would he care?
How could after more than half of her life
They see each other and act as though the other is not there?
How could this be?
He dares to bring a bum around me
And trust I won't commit a felony
Does he see something in her heart that she's missing
Or is it a set-up?
Killing me softly is what she thinks he's trying to do
She's stronger than she knows
Because she amazes herself each time she imagines they're both invisible
She used to think love was real
Not questing another's motives when he said he loved her
Now everything is suspect to her
Now when she looks at people she's automatically guarded
With 21 questions in mind

Does she dare tell she thinks he's messed her up for life?
They vowed till death do us part, and she thinks that's one promise he'll probably keep
He has damaged her heart
She got a life sentence on that day and no one told her that it was suspect
No one told her that her heart might be being set-up
She can't figure out how she can still love someone who is so cold
She can't understand how she still cries for someone that never recognized
The love that was there for them all along
She wonders if ever in this lifetime she will be blessed with real love
She wonders if her eyes will ever sparkle with the thought of a man
A man that's able to be called her man
Who's not afraid to love her the way a man is supposed to love a woman
A man who will allow her to love him
The way a woman is supposed to love a man
The way this woman wants to love her man
She wonders if the day will ever come when she doesn't feel so alone
She's scared to trust anyone for fear of being hurt
But she knows she'll never see brighter days if she doesn't trust
How? is her question
How can she?
She doesn't want to go back
But it hurts her to see him moving on
She's scared to move on
So still she stands
All of it is killing her softly…

My Bahamian Black Man

Where did you come from and where will you go
My Mystery Man?
So quickly you came into my life to leave
I'm in love with my friend
A man of mystery
My Bahamian Black Man
He keeps me intrigued
You've inspired me more than words could ever say
I constantly want more
May I indulge in your secret world?
In my mind I see you in many places
Take me where only you go
Could you be my soul mate
The one I've longed for to open my eyes
Eyes that've been wide shut to many existences?
My equilibrium is off balance when I'm not with you
But then I close my eyes
And all around me you appear
Inhaling I breathe the air you breathe
And the euphoria carries me to where you are
Brilliant beyond measures
Opulent possessing many talents
Haven is what they named him at birth foreseeing the future
Eminence is obvious whenever you're in his presence
Magnetic he is capturing my mind using it as his workshop
Intelligent
Astounding
Noticeable in character and demeanor

These and many other words describe him
My Bahamian Black Man
My Mystery Man
My friend
Wanting to say a lot but scared I'll say too much
I listen and linger on every word you say
Like food and water you nourish my soul
I can only hope the times we've shared have fed you like me
How I'd love to ensoul you
Wanting you to ensoul me
Us to ensoul each other
So that we could experience each other the way no one has before
However...
That might be asking for too much too soon
So I treasure what I have while I have it
Knowing forever is too far away
The end too near
I'm thanking my God each day
For my Bahamian Black Man...
My Mystery Man...
He became My Lover...
He'll always be My Friend...

Confusion

Confused about when, were and why
Should I just be who I am
Or should I live in a world
A state of being
Created by another?
I want to love
I need love
Does it really matter where I get it?
Or does it matter
The source of my contentment for satisfaction?
I suppress so many feelings
To keep from being judged
Judged by those who have no meaning
To me or my life
Why is that?
I want to live in a world where all can be…
A world where I am free to be me
Not worrying about what others think…

Temporary Love

I'm sitting thinking about last night
Overwhelmed by how all of my senses were aroused
Mental stimulation is the best foreplay
I can't explain my feelings
I truly don't even understand them
I've stopped trying and I've succumbed to all that's happening
So little time we have
So much to share
Heaven sent
A fallen angel has come into my life
Ignorant to this type of communion
No one would believe
How elated and blissful my life has become
Even if it is temporary love
I will forever be grateful
I've been allowed to experience the fullness of him
My angel fallen from heaven
A part of me almost wishes we never met
Because of the void that will be left when he's gone
But it's too late for regrets
And truly I have none
I would start over today with whatever it is we share
If I had to do it again
Because I'm sitting thinking about last night
Wishing it never had to end...

Nameless

How do you know if you're falling in love?
It's too soon to even fathom
Oh, but it feels so right
This feeling I have inside
Perfect?
What does that mean?
Maybe the way he says hello
Maybe the way he looks in my eyes
Perhaps it's just the smile I get
Walking by
As he sits talking to another
I can't explain it
Somehow I just know
This man is the one for me
We can sit and not say two words aloud
Silently we've whispered a thousand
Never touching
I can feel the warmth of his body all around me
It's almost inconceivable
The notion
Love at first sight
As he entered the room
Everything else faded
Leaving our eyes to meet and introduce two souls
Two lonely souls awaiting destiny
I'm not one to question
To be is what's meant and vice versa
I just want to know what this feeling is

That's weighing heavy on my heart
Is it love?
Probably not
How can it be?
I don't even know his name...

Hiding Within

Hiding within a safe haven afraid to let go
It's easy to get comfortable inside
Such as a turtle in its shell
Freeing your mind
Opening yourself up to another
Within you feel should be deemed a taboo thought
Why elude yourself?
Deep within you already know it can't be real
However two beings co-existing can become one
Afraid to find out
You seek shelter within
Hibernating…
Mothering your heart
Protecting your feelings from what's conceived to be brash and harsh
Never truly finding out what's real
Why is my heart racing with each thought of this man?
Why am I so anxious
Feeling like I'm suffocating
Within the same walls he's in?
Breathing his air makes me feel faint
But to open myself up
How can I?
How can I fathom trusting another human being with what pumps life into my body?
My soul feels like we're connected
I don't know
Maybe from another life

Maybe I was he and he was I
Destined to meet again
Seeing through eyes that once housed his soul and spirit
Eyes that are so beautiful to me
They glisten like the stars at night
I ponder, what is it that he's doing to me?
That's all I want to know
Every second of each day I'm consumed with thoughts of him
But how can this be?
I don't come out of my shell
I am just like the turtle
Hiding within

No More Room

What am I to do when I am the one that everyone leans on?
I could easily seclude myself behind walls
Walls made of the strongest steel
Walls that could shield me from all the pressures that I face daily
But is isolation the best therapy?
Solitary confinement could drive a person mad
If they aren't warrior material
Built to survive
Spirits lurking in the atmosphere
Preying on souls much like mine
Souls that take on everyone else's pain and grievances
Those spirits could run you away into a secret place
A place you enter all alone
You and you
Left to dwell within
Comforting only you
No one understands how it hurts to be lost within yourself
Afraid to come out because the world wants to rob you of your joy
Steal your face
Like a thief in the night
I am sheltering my face while I weather this storm
Visions of opening up and inviting others into my world
I have often
But there's no more room

Damn, Not Tonight

Wishing I were in my bed
Instead I'm out doing what I have to do
My mother didn't raise me this way
Is often the thought going through my mind
As I feel hot breath breathing over me
People often talk about the struggles they face
Me, I'd rather just get caught up
Caught up in the hustle and bustle to make mine a little easier
A dollar is hard to come by
If you don't know where to look
You can make money and still be "respectable"
Is how I find myself easing my mind when guilt tries to rear his ugly head
My pillow sure would feel good right now
But my bills are pilled way high
The smell of fresh linen is tempting
But my lay-away is due
Please not tonight
Don't spit as you talk
DAMN, is it 2:00 yet?

What Is His Name?

There's something about a man
His touch
When he knows how to soothe the burning
Way down
Deep inside
It's something that you can't resist
The touch of hands so smooth
The feel of lips so soft
A body so hard
The scent of a man
So good
I can't resist this man
I try hard each day
What is his name?
I better not say
But
His hands;
They caress my body
Just the way you would smooth a newborn's hair
Soft and gentle
His fingers
He runs them over my body nice and slow
From my neck
Along my spine he loses me with his touch
As I slip into a euphoric state awaiting his kisses
I can't resist this man
I try hard each day
What is his name?

I better not say
His lips are like *dope*
Sending me on a high *with each kiss*
My pulse quickens
Thinking about the way our tongues dance with each other
It's getting hot in here
Hum
But maybe it's just me
Because his face is all I see
I can't resist this man
I try hard each day
What is his name?
I better not say
A body so hard—oh shit—
I'm holding on tight
As he takes me on a ride
AND he's doing it right
He's sculpted from head to toe
Chiseled like a fine piece of art
He's moving like a cheetah in the wind
Body perfect
Glistening like the sun has dropped honey from heaven over his bronzed skin
Dammit
I can't resist this man
I try hard each day
What is his name?
I better not say
Now there's nothing better than a man who smells good
You smell him
I see you
And I'm wishing you would
Um as I lay next to him as he's holdin' me tight

I breathe in————long and hard
And close my eyes tight
I'm engaged in my brain
Over all the things this man does to me
Captivated I'm contemplating on how to be set free
His hands work magic
You'd swear they weren't real
His lips they arouse—and they bring you so near
His body without fail brings me to a point of climax where
Damn, together with his scent
Is so good!
I can't resist this man
I try hard each day
What is his name?
Ladies, I can't…
I mean…
I better not say!

A Player

He said I once was a player
Huh?
A player
Huh?
A player
A player he still is to me
He wouldn't stop until
He saw me cream
Be mad
How can I
I allowed him
Between my thighs?
Now I sit
Watching him woo someone else's eyes
A smooth operator he is
Silk can't touch his style
I still love to see his smile
He warmed my heart
If only for one night
He won't stop
Until he finishes his plight
I once was a player
Is what he told me
Me he never again will see
A player he was
Tight with his game
But
He'll never forget my name!

I Need a Breakthrough

I need a breakthrough
My struggles are almost too hard to bear
Someone please help me through this storm
Because right now I'm in a state of mind
Where
Despair is all I see
I'm trying to keep from breaking the law
It's getting harder and harder by the second
What is one to do when bill collectors are constantly calling left and right?
I vow to myself not to break
Faking like I can handle the pressure
I have several options
All of which are illegal
But this is some bullshit
Something's got to give
Working 9-5 just ain't getting the job done
And hell, it's just me
I could probably work round the clock from sunrise to sunset
But dammit, what about me?
Where do I fit into this fucked-up picture?
Ms. Always trying to do right, don't want to do wrong
Willing to help anybody, and owe everybody
Can't get no help
Where is time for me?
Working like a Hebrew slave still ain't cutting the slack
Maybe I should just get a few rocks
Or go down the street and take my clothes off for a few hours a night

Then I'm sure I could see the light
But
That wouldn't be respectable
However, I would get respect
Who the hell am I fooling?
It's all about the almighty dollar out here flat out
People respect money, period
They don't give a damn how holy you are
Or how "good" you try to be
You will just be another broke b out here
And fuck that shit, cause that's me
Been working hard for years
Seventeen of them and often times holding down at least two jobs,
Sometimes three
But a broke b I be now you tell me
What ain't right about this picture?
When I could be out here hustlin' like the next playa
Workin' my hand stayin' fly
Hell I can't even afford a new pair of shoes—it's pitiful
Sometimes I cry,
"Lord, why me?
What have I done so terribly wrong in life?"
I believe in Karma so I say it must be I'm paying for a past life
Because my struggle is never ending
Thank God I don't have kids because we wouldn't make it
We couldn't
If I can't put milk in my mouth, how could I put it in theirs?
Lord please hear my cry
This is too much to bear
I need someone to lighten up on this noose around my neck
I'm choking about to gag
Lord you know I don't want to pull a trick out my bag
Drug dealin', strippin', boostin', what have you

In a minute I'm gone have to go for what I know
In the hood we gone get ours one way or the other
Lord I'm cryin' out to you
Please see my struggle
Have mercy on your child who's trying to do right and don't want to do wrong
Help me my Father to just Hold On!

Are You Ready?

The necessary things in life are often times difficult
But if you let your soul lead you, you will make it through
Our ancestors have all tread down roads we find ourselves going down today
How did they survive?
How did they see it through?
Spiritual hymns often soothed their souls
Of the scars that were left from wounds dug deep
Praises to our Lord and Savior went up
Blessings from the man above came flowing down
Today a lot of us tend to turn to tranquilizers that are very detrimental to our health
Drugs…sex…violence…
All roads with dead-ends
I once heard someone say
That you should look into your heart with a positive mind
Take *self* inventory…leave the bad things behind
But,
Are you ready?
Because when you're ready I will appear
That's what I heard him say to me one day
So I closed my eyes and looked within
All the while listening to his voice
All that you seek you shall have
But first you must be willing to let go
Freeing your mind so that your subliminal state
Can come together with your soul and spirit
Thus, bringing forth revelations you knew not even existed

Is it by chance that suddenly you're faced with thoughts and ideas of me?
That may or may not be true
But ideas that've been implanted in your mind over time
Making this process of revelation more difficult than imagined
Begin to look deeper
Check out each feeling
Weigh your emotions
It will help bring clarity for truly clarity is what you seek
While weeding through what's been planted in your mind
This is a fragile process
But one that cannot be escaped for the truth you will find once complete
When you're ready
Searching I found—substitutions I needed no more
False promises
Illusive sense of securities
Lying and cheating all coming to the surface now
I needed no more
Subjective thoughts from those so beneath me; beneath what I stood for
I needed no more
"Search deeper, my child," I heard him say
"Cut through the layers
Get to the core of your every being
Clean it up…let it go."
Preconceived notions that I was less than I was—surfacing
I needed no more
Sitting in silence meditating on my creator he showed me
"You are like the moon and the stars
For your light shines brighter than any I've created
Burning in you as the sun, is a word
A word I've given you for the world to hear

Through you I will speak and all will listen
Through you, my diligent one, I will give visions and share dreams
Just continue to seek my face and hear my voice
Mistaking mine for none other
Listening to me, you won't have to go where others have gone
Because you will know the way
Once you're ready."
Lingering on every thought
I closed my eyes again asking myself
Is there a comparison?
To whom should you run when you seek a solemn place?
Whose breath can you breathe?
Whose touch can stop the trembles?
Whose heartbeat, slow rhythm can ensnare, engulf your every existence?
Then I heard
"Is it mine that you seek?
My comforting spirit?"
Opening my eyes in my spirit I said, "Yes,
Yes, I am,"
Though I thought I was not
To you, maybe
To them, who cares?
Love is good, courageous, and outstanding
Love endures all bitterness, pain, longsuffering, and evil
The voice I heard was love
At that moment I knew…
Yes, I'm ready…

The Game of Life

Sitting back and feeling sad
I'm not
Although I don't know which way to turn or what to do
My walls are bare—picture free
I guess giving my brain time to let it sink in
Old memories are fading away
New memories will be created one day
All the things man can supply you'll have again
Materialistic things
The luxuries of living in a society where
People are judged by how much they have
Not how much good they do
You'll get again
Right now is "healing" time
Time that's been given to me
To allow my insides to be completely cleansed
From all the dirt that's been allowed to build up over so many years
"Tainted" I'll be no more
In time
Huh? "In time," that's all I used to think I heard
From those who had it all
In time you'll have a couch
Coming from someone who's not sitting on the floor
In time you'll have a TV
Again, from someone not watching the bare walls
Sitting alone, I couldn't help but to reminisce on old times
Times filled with beautiful pictures that were on my walls

Not all were bad
But certainly not all were good
Such is life
Which is why I know that I have more than most people have
Given the existing circumstances
That is a peace of mind
I truly feel I have been given one of the greatest gifts a person could receive
And that is knowledge combined with wisdom
The wisdom to know what this world is truly about
Why me?
Why me?
Why me?
That's what I used to ask
What was done so wrong that I deserve this?
Haven't I tried to live by the golden rule?
Sure as a child I did childlike things
But being an adult I have always thought of others
Thought of the consequences for my actions
Limited the amount of fulfillment I would receive
To ensure not stepping on anyone else's heart
People smile in your face all day long
A cover-up
To me life is one big set-up
The *major game*
No one truly has your back out here
Because everyone has to cover their own
Very easy for someone to get caught up
Caught up trying to come up
It's funny but this is the world we are living in
You're made to believe you should live a certain way
Be Christ-like
It's better to give than to receive

A bunch of *bullshit*
This is a dog-eat-dog world
Period…Dot
Everyone out here is trying to come up
Fuck what you heard
That's why I say it's a set up
You ain't taught the real deal as a kid
As a kid they teach you to go to school
Be nice
Get good grades
Go to college so you can get a good job
Get married
Have kids
And live happily ever after…
Psyche!
That's all Hollywood drama, save it fo' yo' mama
It's rough in the hood believe what I tell you
And people can't wait to kick you when you are already down on the curb
But you know what?
A 'b' like me already knows what time it is
Survival of the fittest is the name of the game
Everyone might be laughing now
But they need to watch out
It won't be long before it's on and poppin' like a bag of popcorn
You can't hold me down because it's in my blood to come up
Some way…some how
No they won't understand it
But then they must not really and truly understand the Game
This is "Life"
Live
It
Fuck
Em!

Redemption Song

When loneliness sets in
It feels almost like death
Creeping into my bones
Suffocating within these four walls
The ceiling is lowering
Floor rising
I am lost within myself
Hurting to the point
I feel I am losing my mind
Please just stop the agony
Is my constant prayer
Because the tears won't stop falling
Drowning I ask myself
How did it come to this?
I try so hard to deny
I am slowly dying inside
Being alone is killing me
But staying was killing me too
The music is so loud in the membranes of my brain
I can remember every note played on that day
The day you vowed to love me only
Till death do us part
The day you took my heart in your hands
And played with it like a yo-yo
I really thought I meant more to you than that
I always knew you'd change
But you let me slip away
Now I'm lost in the wilderness

In a world full of strangers
When the only man I loved
Is oh so far away
"How did it come to this?" I cry
I tried so hard to be right
In a world full of wrong doings
Only the strong survive, is what they say
Which is why I feel I have lost
Because my soul is weakened
From all the pain and hurt
I've been cut before
But the piercing of a knife through your heart
It's unbearable
My soul has been captured by the enemy
Who does not want to turn it loose
I cry out to my Lord for redemption
Because I know he's the only one who can save me now
"Help me, Lord!" I cry
I can take no more
I'm drowning in my own tears
Tears the other part of me have caused to fall endlessly
Save me from this untimely death of misery
Heal my once-unbroken heart
Help me to love again teach me to trust again
Because right now I'm lost inside a shell
The sun went down one day
And never came back out
Lord shine your light on me

Overjoyed

No one could possibly understand
The magnitude of joy I feel
Unless they were inside this vessel
Encapsulated within me
The fullness I feel in my heart
I've never felt for another
I now know how Juliet felt about her Romeo
Bonnie about her Clyde
For the love of my life
I've found in you
No one could ever come in between it
If I could tap my heels and wish to go home
My spirit would join yours
And they would intertwine like vines at a vineyard
Never to part
Our love would grow stronger and stronger
With the electricity we'd both bring
How you pull at my heart
No one could possibly understand
Leaving a tornado
I've found the calm after the storm in you
Forever in my eyesight you'll be my pillar of strength
My solid rock to lean on
A cake is not complete
Without carefully measuring the sugar
And adding the eggs
One by one
Neither is my life without you in it

Careful not to give too much at one time
But definite to give it all
Never will I leave your side
I'll be your diamond
Forever to shine
Princess cut and flawless fit just for you
It's been a long time coming
But no more will I search
For heaven has knocked at my door and placed your hand in mine
We'll cross the line together becoming husband and wife
Defying all odds we'll stand
Creating our own destiny
Going against what others thought to be impossible
Creating magical moments
Outlining a blueprint designed for endless love
Living in the now
Preparing for the future
Names illuminated like the stars at night
Yours and mine
No one could possibly understand
How what was not supposed to be
Can be
How the love between two people so far apart
Can grow so strong and pull them
So close together
In bitter cold
I feel nothing but warmth
The happiness from my heart overflows
Seeping through my pores
Causing everyone around me to stare
On fire for you—my love
No one could possibly understand
How this feeling I feel takes over my body

My mind
My soul
Causing me to put on blinders to everything else
Lose sight of me
And only see one thing—Us
No one could possibly understand
How overjoyed I am to have you
No one could possibly understand…

Something on My Heart

There's something on my heart I need to say
You inspire me every day
Life may not be perfect for me
But it is very far from being incomplete
You've helped me through many tough times
That is why it is so difficult to get you off my mind
Beautiful you are to me
I feel like a bird that has been set free
Happiness is in the air
You can smell the aroma everywhere
There's something on my heart I need to say
I'm loving you more and more each day
You can liken this feeling to jubilee
That's what you do for me
As bright as the stars shine at night
As beautiful as the sun is by day
Everywhere I turn
Everywhere I look
I see your face
I smile with every thought of you
To you I will forever be true
There's something on my heart I need to say
I'm loving you so much this day
Have you ever witnessed a cup just overflow
So much has been poured into it, it has nowhere to go
Such is my heart with the joy you've given me
It's like you've placed it under lock-n-key
I can only pray I've given you the same

One day I say, I'll wear his name
For you see, I can only see one thing in the future
That's me and you
Like I told you before
To you I will forever be true
There's something on my heart I need to say
I love you each second
Each minute
Each hour
With every breath that I take of each day
I love you…

To Dream

To dream is to long for something so intensely
And to imagine it coming to pass
However, for me, I dream not for a man
For you have come into my life and made it complete
Concentration is a rare thing for me these days
Because you creep into my thoughts morning, noon and night
Just as a thief
You steal my dreams and invade my brain
Compelling me to see only your face
I am stifled by your smell that forever surrounds me
Making it often times difficult to breathe
I kiss your face in my sleep
I make love to your ever so masculine body during the day
As I touch myself, I am consumed with thoughts of you
Thoughts which cause me to climax and produce orgasms
That generate hollow moans and sudden cries
Only you could masterfully create
Craving for you till my insides yearn stronger and stronger
How I long to feel the touch of your hands on my skin…
The feel of your lips on my breasts…
Your tongue on my nipples…
Your hard manhood inside my walls
Walls that are empty
Waiting patiently for you to paint your picture on
Just as Leonardo Da Vinci created Mona Lisa
You are the food I long to eat
Making my every existence even possible
For you cause the blood to flow through my body

Energizing my soul
I am complete until the moment you escape my thoughts
Then for you I dream again

Man in the Mirror

In search of oneself
You must be willing to truly face the man in the mirror
Illusions often persuade your opinion
Focus and seek clarity
In my personal search for oneself
I've gone through many different horizons
Over my own hurdles created by demons within
In casting those demons out
I have reflected back to my own mirror
Seeking my face, my spirit, my soul
Depth of one's soul can fade into pictures of prudence
Eluding your inner-being
Be true to yourself
If you're not true to self, to whom will you be true?
You'll find masking your real face
Will lead you down a path that's sure to be full of lies and deceit
Reality will soon fade, and you will be left wondering
How you got on a road that seems never-ending
A road you want to get off, but you're so caught up
How did your mama tell you?
You made your bed, now lie in it
It may be a hard one, but those are the breaks
Self preservation is the law of nature
However, does that defy one's God-given right to
Love thy neighbor as thyself?
If you know who you are you can treat all people equally
You can preserve self and still not be afraid to trust others
In finding ourselves we will learn how far to go

We will learn that truly we are not as needy as we feel we are
God has blessed us all with everything we need within ourselves
That's why it is so important to evaluate ourselves
And truly analyze critically, not being afraid to look in the mirror
It's true you may not always like what you see
But then you have the option of change
Be willing
Because truly it is when you're not even compelled
Or lead to search out your true inner man
That you should be afraid
Now you're talking about living a life never knowing who you really are
A life never knowing who God really blessed you to be
Never developing talents that we all possess
Talents God gave us
To be used, nourished and fed
So I say again
Search out yourself
Look for the man in the mirror
He will appear…

Silent Whispers

As you close your eyes
And your soul travels to places outside of your physical body
Listen closely for my silent whispers
There you will find the secrets of my heart left unspoken
My innermost feelings that I'm no longer afraid to share with you
As we meet in our secret garden
When you feel a slight breeze on the back of your neck
It is only I
Blowing ever so lightly
As your scent comes back and consumes me
The tingling down your spine
Lets you know I am there
Prepare to listen
For silently I will begin to whisper the secrets of my heart
Do you share any of these secrets?
You tell me
For you should know the answer by now
I have been talking silently to you for some time
More than a decade ago our conversation started
Many a night I have shared with you
My soul mate
Becoming one, transparent to the naked eye
To imagine you with me
Longing intensely to see your face
I speak silently to your heart
From my heart to yours I whisper my secret desires
To love you in ways only I can love you
Silent whispers I am almost afraid to speak

If only you could see into my heart
You'd keep me close knowing I'd keep you warm when it's cold
Forever willing to satisfy your needs
Giving you sunshine on your bluest day
These are silent whispers spoken with so much passion
In your dreams you awaken in a cold sweat anticipating the moment
You allow yourself to be captivated with my unspoken words of desire
Willing to free your mind of forbidden fantasies
To meet me on the other side
Where our silent whispers can be heard
Secretly you speak back
Opening up a whole other side of yourself that you're only willing to share with me
I ain't mad at you because secretly, I don't want anyone else to know
This is my whisper
It is my turn
To silently fulfill your needs
Erotic
Emotional
Physical
Mental
You whisper thoughts of you and I you envision
That take you back to our garden
Where I yearn to meet you every night
Thoughts that secretly I've been having myself for sometime
How can two people share the same thought?
Two people in two bodies
With one vision
One purpose
One goal

One destiny
One thought that silent whispers have allowed to grow secretly in
our hearts
That is how two people secretly become one
Two people like you and I
For silent whispers have told all

Inspired

My inspiration comes from the stillness of the night
From birds flying high
From rivers running low
My inspiration comes from the unspoken words you keep hidden inside
Words spoken through spirits not heard by human ears
When winds blow silently as raindrops fall
In a corner nestled with pen and paper I write
Being inspired by each drop trickling down my window pane
Wisdom cometh from deep within
This is the wisdom that keeps me going
Driven to search out my next source of inspiration
Listening with great intent
Lingering on to each vowel and syllable you speak
I am inspired
Such passion I see in your eyes
Eyes brown as the soil of the earth
Deep as the greatest bodies of water
I am inspired
How could one be so perfect?
Made by a creator we all long to be like
I am inspired to seek out him who made us all
To walk as he once walked
To speak as he once spoke
To see beauty as he saw beauty in every living thing
In the birds
In the trees
In the most beautiful of flower

In the foulest smell in the air
In his sight all things are made perfect
I am inspired
My every source of inspiration comes from the man upstairs
Who sits high and reigns low
I am inspired because he has given me so many things
To look upon and dream for
Each day I wake
I am inspired

Sir Rob

CHARACTER, STRENGTH, WISDOM
His stature is that of a mountain
Eyes those of an eagle soaring high
His strength is like Samson
They call him Sir Rob
Nine plus bullets can't stop a man
Who is destined to do great things
Towering like a pillar above most
I see **100% Black Man**
A brotha, true in every sense of the word…
Laying low like a cheetah in the cut
He sits back and watches all haters
People try to bring you down
When they see greatness
But guess what…Can't stop, won't stop
Is the attitude built in
Ready to attack if need be
Always peepin' game
Fake is a word that would never be used
To describe the man I see
100% Black Man—Sir Rob is what they call him
Loyal to those that deserve loyalty
Ruthless to all enemies
A lover and a friend to his one and only "Baby Boo"
A side all you haters will never see
A side that "Sir Rob" has for only me

Love Anew

I am all woman and you are all man
Like Hillary and Bill Clinton, what a pair
But, just like summer ends and fall begins
Just has our love for a new
Realizing that everything desirable was your queen
How you now long to taste my sweet nectar
Like a bee stealing from a precious flower
But, my venom is like a poisonous snake
For my heart has turned cold like ice
100% woman waiting to serve 100% man
What can cause this combination to sour?
Temptation makes the pulse quicken and mind go blank
Temptation can make a husband forget his wife
And likewise
But
When this 100% woman joins together with her 100% man
Inseparable we will be
When this 100% woman joins together with her 100% man
We will be on a one-way highway to destiny
Close your eyes and envision moments in love
Together we will try to find infinity
You and I
On a journey searching for endless love
Never-ending

When Our Souls Meet

Thoughts of yesterday forever stay on my mind
Reminiscing of the times you and I once shared
Some would say; look, they're so in love
You know, eyes tell it all
Secret rendezvous were commonplace for us
We would get in where we fit in so to speak
How I long today to just have you near me
Any way I can
To feel the touch of your skin against mine
Hypnotic...
To have your lips meet mine
Tranquilizing...
When our eyes meet
The journey we've both been on to complete what we started
So many years ago, will be over
The depths of our souls will ignite
Passion flames will be impossible to put out
When your soul meets mine
I'll let you know you're home
When your soul meets mine
We'll be makin' good love all night long
When your soul meets mine
The heat will be turned up, temperatures will rise
When your soul meets mine
You'll be livin' in between these thighs

Serendipity

Listen to the wind blow
The rustle of the leaves
Have you ever wondered what the crickets are chirping about at night
Or the birds in the morning?
Can you understand their conversation
In the still of the moment
A voice can be heard
Can you hear it?
Do you understand what's being said?
Sirens sound off
Engines start up
Train horns blow; all outside the walls of my serene place
Serenity…Peace…Solace…
I have finally found them all
I can listen to the creatures of nature
Hear their conversations
I can hear the rustling of the leaves
And the hustle and bustle of life
Then I can hear the peace that surrounds me
Listening to raindrops fall
I hear peace
The birds singing their songs in the morning
I hear peace
Cars going past to each of their destinations
I hear peace
Peace in its purest form
Spoken so beautifully, it fills my heart with joy

Staring
I look at one of God's most beautiful creations
A pale blue sky
Endless beauty
Endless peace
Endless amounts of opportunity
What's really out there for me to see across a sky that runs like a river
Symbolizing infinity?
I've found peace here in my solemn place with my birds, and trees, and crickets at night
BUT
What are the birds sounding like out there?
Maybe somewhere out there, awaits for me a little piece of heaven
Maybe somewhere out there my soul mate waits
Wishing on a star for me
Just as I am for him
Maybe when I stare into the clouds
Listening to the music made by my birds
He's staring at the same cloud listening to his
Our souls calling for one another
To complete the missing link between peace and heaven
How I long to meet somewhere
Where butterflies fly across fields of flowers that smell sweet like honey
Where the aroma takes you to a place, only lovers are allowed to go
Across skies so clear
You know you're in a place far from here
Where we can be free to love the way forbidden lovers do
Two soul's peaceful coming together to solidify the link
That has been missing between the two; the link between peace and heaven

Two souls longing for just a touch of heaven
That can only be created when destiny joins them together…
Serendipity…

Only You

Only you could understand the emptiness
I feel inside when I close my eyes
And dream of yesterday

Laughter sounding like it's appeared
From the depths of a belly
So full of joy

Remembering the times we once shared
Brings butterflies back to my stomach
The way they were there
Each time before we made passionate love

Umm the lovemaking
"Good" does it no justice
Just the thought of you entering me
Makes my temperature rise
Like the mercury inside a thermometer

Only you could know what I see
When I close my eyes and in my mind
I travel years back in time
To a place you and I once shared
Moments we created
Our time
Our yesteryear

Those were times our history books were made of
Only you would know what I mean
It's funny how two people can share so much
So many memories
And walk away from it all
Like nothing has taken place

But
Only you can fill that spot in my heart
That you put your name on so long ago
Only you can make me laugh
The way I laughed so long ago
Only you can make me smile
The way I smiled so long ago
Only you

Hurting

Why do I feel so sad?
Why am I so blue?
I did everything that a wife is supposed to for her husband,
Yet I am the one with hurt feelings and mixed emotions.
Had I known that going through a relationship
With someone that I loved,
And who claimed to love me too, would leave me feeling this way,
I doubt if I ever would have agreed to such a commitment.
I truly feel empty!
It actually feels worse than when someone dies,
At least then you can still smile and laugh a bit.
I don't have any laughter within.
I have no one to share my pain with.
I keep telling myself,
That this has to be where I am supposed to be right now in my life,
However,
I don't know how I am going to make it through.
Feeling the way that I feel right now,
I feel like I need medication for depression…
I can barely write;
I can barely crack a fake smile.
All I really want to do is sit and stare.
Stare into my past and see if I can see where I went wrong.
Stare into the future and see if ever I'll be able to smile again.
Wonder if anyone cares how I am really feeling.
Wishing someone would come hug some of my pain away.
Emptiness is not a fun feeling.
No good at all…

Shallow would describe best the feeling inside me.
Like a shallow grave dug for someone…
The someone that once housed this body of mine.
My soul…
Because it feels as though it has left me…
Here empty inside…
Hurting, to cry endlessly.

Friend

From beginning to end
Regardless of the situation
In every passing breath
Endless love abounds
Never to be forgotten
Destined to be friends

Breathless

In the morning when I rise
With sleep still in my eyes
Your face appears just like the sun after a spring shower
Before the rainbow fades

Breathless is the feeling that overcomes me
With the very thought of your smile
The look in your eyes when you stare back at me
Silent whispers, only we can interpret
Breathless as the thought of our lips touching
I think to myself
These are all reasons why I love you

Maybe it's the feeling I have
As you slowly creep into my dreams day and night
Now as dawn turns to dusk
And the moonlight does its dance on my pillow
Before me is a frame that houses a spirit so much like mine
A soul yearning to be loved just as mine

Again breathless
I am overcome by the electricity I feel
That's generated between you and me
You and this thing I feel
Deep inside me…stirring and brewing, like a volcano
About to erupt

As you appear once more before me

As I kneel before the stars
Helpless I fight to control my emotions
As I yearn to feel your touch, see your smile, read your eyes

Your eyes
They talk to me just as a child talks to his mother
Just learning to babble
I often wonder if mine say the same

Not only am I breathless, you're breathless too

Past, Present, Future

She often dreamed and at times I know she'd reminisce
Where did the time go, what did she miss?
Thoughts of yesterday clouded her vision
Now she sits and questions,
Did I make the right decision?
He was gone and now she's all alone
Was it worth it?
She had let him go to complete someone else's home
He was her yesterday
Her today is full of sorrow,
Someone please tell her
What does she have to look forward to tomorrow?
Sleepless nights she has
She tosses and turns
Deep down inside for him she yearns.
Lord knows she's cried and many days she hated him too…
But look at her now,
To whom does she turn?
What must she do?
He was her everything…like ice cream completes cake
Someone please tell her…has she made a terrible mistake?
Why did she let him go and complete someone else's home?
Now here she sits, all alone
She tries to go on as though he never existed
A tough role she tries to play
But the truth of the matter is,
Yes he did exist
He was her every existence…

Her everything...
Her King...
Her Hero...
Her Lover...
Her Man...
Her Husband...
Their Everything...
Their Lover...
Their Undercover Man...
Her HOE!
Oops, what? He thought she didn't know!
You see all those nights she cried, and she was missing him too
She knew he was with them,
Thrusting deep inside them,
Calling them his Boo!
That's why when she sits here and she thinks about the times that
the two of them shared
I really can't understand why she was so scared.
Scared of letting go
Scared everyone would know
That really the man she had married,
Was nothing but a HOE!
She's still a bit confused,
Because you see, while she was sexing him down good
Licking him from the top of his head to the soles of his feet and
everywhere in between,
Loving him till her love juices were flowing down his magic stick
like water at the
Grand Canyon
Turning him around and sucking him until
Umm...she'd tasted all his Honeydew...How could he go and call
Them...call *anyone* besides her, his Boo?
Was it something she had done?

Hell no…
Oh yeah she forgot,
He was just a HOE!
So now when she dreams and she reminisces,
She no longer questions what did I do? What did I miss?
Now when she sits she thinks Past, Present, Future
Really she must "Thank You" for being an excellent tutor.
They say life's lessons are hard to learn
A PhD in Psychology, **Pimp**ology, **Hoe**ology she'd have to say she has earned.
He was an excellent example of the type of man not to have…
A pre-requisite for the real thing she guesses someone felt she must have.
Thoughts of yesterday once clouded her vision
But now its time for her to close that incision.
Why did she go and let you complete someone else's home…
Because in her Kingdom…her Heavenly place…you did not belong!

Lover's Voodoo

I breathe in…he breathes out
Until we're breathing as one
The rhythm that we have is so harmonious
It's like an orchestra at a Beethoven concert
Slow and easy….Yeah, that's the way tonight
Until his lips touch mine…
Then my pulse quickens
Mmm…it's so good
The short quick breaths I take
Breathing in all the aroma from our beautiful lovemaking
His body so hard and masculine,
Mine soft as a baby's behind
Wet as the grass after the morning dew
Mmm…what is this he's doing to me?
I can barely take it…
It must be called Lover's Voodoo

Monday

Monday has come…oh that dreaded Monday
The beginning of another week
40 hours of my life given to someone else
Goodbye weekend
But what does Monday really signify?
The **Beginning**
A *New* day
Life…starting anew
Another day to smell fresh air
Another day to step on new ground
Another day to be a *new and better me!*
Thank God, it's Monday!

I Am

I am what I am, and that's all that I am
Nothing more, nothing less
I am God's creation.

Tell me you want a housewife
And I will show you me
Tell me you want a whore
And I will show you me

I have no standards to uphold…Why?

Because I am what I am, and that's all that I am
Nothing more, nothing less
I am God's creation

Black, beautiful, and proud
I see in the mirror everyday
Battered, broken-hearted and teary-eyed
In my bed I lay

Yet, I still have no standards to uphold…Why?

Because I am what I am, and that's all that I am
Nothing more, nothing less
I am God's creation

Show me a Conqueror
I will say, "that's me"

Show me Courage
I will say, "that's me"
Strong-willed and at peace, **that would be me**

Why?

Because I am what I am, and that's all that I am
Nothing more, nothing less
I am God's creation.

It Won't Go Un-noted

It won't go un-noted
The work that you've done

You will be rewarded for
The problems you've overcome

Just stay strong and stand
I'll be your guiding hand

It won't go un-noted
The work that you've done

About the Author

A Toledo, Ohio native, Isa, who was born Isa Nicole Motley, has been writing since her early teenage years. A music lover and inspired by many phenomenal artists, Isa receives a lot of her inspiration from many talents in the music industry such as Kenneth "Babyface" Edmunds and Lyfe Jennings, to name a few, talents whose writing skills are exceptional and raw. As well, many great authors and poets such as the renowned Maya Angelou have been great inspirations. One of four siblings, Isa also attributes her motivation to the upbringing received by her parents, the late John H. Motley, Jr., and her mother Bernice C. Motley, who still resides in Toledo, Ohio, along with her three siblings. Currently residing in Brownstown Township, Michigan, Isa spends most of her time writing and as much of her time as she can with family and friends. *Tilling the Soul* is Isa's debut publication, and she is currently working on the release of her second, entitled *No Substitutions,* which she hopes to have completed by mid to late 2008.